Airplane Etiquette

Airplane Etiquette

A Guide to Traveling with Manners

PETER SHEARDY

Copyright © 2015 **Authored by Peter Sheardy**
All rights reserved.

ISBN 10: 1508858381
ISBN 13: 9781508858386

Introduction

IF YOU WANT to see the breakdown of the human condition, I spend a day traveling through the airport. I spend my fair share of time there (over one hundred airport interactions a year). Travel is all about movement—driving to the airport, moving through the airport, getting on the plane, moving through the air, getting off the plane, and moving through the airport again. I find that most people are oblivious to the process of "movement." They are unaware that there are thousands of other people attempting to do the same thing, to get somewhere.

I have been a road warrior, actually an "air warrior," for over twelve years. I have been in the elite travel programs for six different airlines, been through 164 domestic airports, and, at my pinnacle, stayed 242 nights in a hotel in one year. One whirlwind trip took me from Pittsburg, Pennsylvania, to New York City, New York, to Lansing, Michigan, to Lafayette, Louisiana, to Greensboro, North Carolina, and then back to Pittsburgh on four different airlines, all in four days! The highlight of that trip was lost luggage from Lansing to Lafayette. It was finally delivered to me about one hour before my outbound flight, which was on a different airline.

My point is that I feel that I am qualified to write this book about the process of getting somewhere. But more importantly, getting somewhere with proper etiquette! So I bring you: *Airplane Etiquette: A Guide to Traveling with Manners*.

This book is a revelation, an illumination, a realization, a self-help, a how-to—and a book of bad examples. But mostly it is a guide. It is for the amateur flier, the novice, and the expert. In fact, sometimes there is a fine line between the amateur and the expert when it comes to etiquette. It is also for the airline industry. Because after all, etiquette begins at home.

If I happen to hand you one of these books while you are engaged in the travel process, don't be offended. It's like somebody handing you a breath mint. Take the subtle hint.

Contents

    Introduction · v
1   Fashion for Flying · · · · · · · · · · · · · · · · · · 1
2   Packing for Security · · · · · · · · · · · · · · · · · 9
3   Driving at the Airport · · · · · · · · · · · · · · · 13
4   Curbside Unloading · · · · · · · · · · · · · · · · 17
5   Ticket Counter Experience · · · · · · · · · · · · 21
6   Moving through Security · · · · · · · · · · · · · 27
7   Moving through the Airport · · · · · · · · · · · · 31
8   Boarding Areas · · · · · · · · · · · · · · · · · · · 35
9   Boarding the Aircraft · · · · · · · · · · · · · · · 39
10 Gate Checking · · · · · · · · · · · · · · · · · · · 43
11 Moving Through the Aircraft · · · · · · · · · · · 47
12 Stowing Luggage · · · · · · · · · · · · · · · · · · 51
13 The Preflight Lecture · · · · · · · · · · · · · · · · 55
14 The In-Flight Experience · · · · · · · · · · · · · · 59
15 Final Approach · · · · · · · · · · · · · · · · · · · 63
16 The Disembarking Process · · · · · · · · · · · · · 67
17 Baggage Claim · 71

18	Curbside Loading	75
	The Arriving Passenger	77
	The Pickup Driver	78
19	Conclusion	79

Appendix

Airline Clubs	81
Parking Lots	82
Shuttles	83
Airports	84
Delayed/Canceled Flights	89
Children on Airplanes	91
Elderly and Assisted Fliers	91
Flight Attendant Faux Pas	92

1

Fashion for Flying

THE FIRST LEG of your travel experience will take you from your home to the terminal doors. You will initialize travel etiquette and travel efficiencies and start to embrace a respect for your fellow travelers. A great place to start is with how you look. I don't mean physical attributes but rather what you wear. Let's get started with some fashion tips for flying.

In the early days of commercial air travel, people dressed for the occasion; ladies wore dresses and hats, while men sported suits and polished shoes. And that was not for going on a business trip; it was just to go visit Aunt Sally! I am sorry to say that today the fashions I see on airplanes are a lot more relaxed than in the past. You still get a smart look from professionals going on business trips, and some vacationers have a casual, social look. But all it takes is one "mutt," and you lose track of fashion sense.

It has been said that "you dress for success" and that "clothes make the person." If that is the case, then some of you are destined for failure. You don't have to go back to the days of ascots and pillbox hats, but you also don't need to look like you just stepped out of the smelter or off of the barroom floor. Remember, you are traveling with fellow passengers. If you dress appropriately, you will look good. If you look good, you will feel good. And when you feel good, so do your fellow travelers.

I travel for business most of the time. My line of work does not require me to wear a suit and tie. However, I don dress slacks and a collared shirt or a dress-type sweater or turtleneck. When I am flying for leisure, guess what? I wear jeans or shorts and a collared shirt. In the wintertime, I might wear a sweatshirt. By the way, none of the clothes I wear have rips or holes in them, and they don't say inappropriate things on them, like "I got drunk and puked at Mack's Bar," or something that can't possibly be true, like "I'm a sex god, and I can last all night," or something absolutely nobody cares about, like "I work out at Big Al's Gym." In case you are wondering, I have seen all of these and more, much more. People put the most inane stuff on clothing and then proudly display it to the rest of humankind. If you have ever looked into the T-shirt windows of Duval Street in Key West, the Grand Strand in Myrtle Beach, or Bourbon Street in New Orleans, those are the kinds of slogan shirts that should *not* be worn on an airplane. Now, if the shirt just said "Mack's Bar" or "Big Al's Gym," that would be acceptable as a form of complimentary advertising and would not be offensive to most people. I was on a flight where a Florida Gators fan thought the guy across from him had on an offensive shirt. It said, "Crimson Tide."

Now, what to wear or what not to wear? That is the question. It will be easier to suggest what *not* to wear, as that list is considerably shorter. I'll start from the ground up.

Footwear: The choice of footwear is usually not as obnoxious as clothes farther up the body. The exception is if you wear sandals and have butt-ugly feet. I mean feet that would make cowboy boots hit the dusty trail. Feet so ugly that running shoes keep on running (away). You know who you are. Hide those bad boys. Don't share them with the other passengers. Some of them may have just eaten. On a flight one time, the guy across the aisle from me was wearing Birkenstocks. Now, his feet weren't ugly, but they had not seen a bar of soap since *The Jackie Gleason Show*! Thank God I wasn't downwind. Which leads me to etiquette: if you have stinky feet, do us all a favor and leave your footwear on. (I know you have to take them off for security, but please, leave them on while aboard the aircraft.) On another occasion, a man came on board wearing waffle-bottomed work boots. He had managed to get from the cow-pie infested field, through the terminal, and onto the plane with a fair amount of "field souvenirs" still clinging to his boots. Come on, Tex. Would you walk into your own living room like that? Maybe he would...

It has been recommended to wear shoes that tie on. This is because if you ever have to vacate the airplane in an emergency situation, a slip-on shoe or sandal or flip-flop could come off in the chaos, thus exposing your feet to potentially painful run-ins.

Ankle to the waist: A while back, a woman was denied entry onto an aircraft because the airline representative deemed she was dressed "too provocatively." That may be a judgment call, but I do suggest this—dress for self-respect. Airplane cabins, for the most part, are not pickup clubs full of desperate people. Now, I have seen relationships cultivated on planes, complete with cocktails, giggling, and some Hoover-like oscillation. However, the rest of the cabin was not impressed with the porno-movie wannabes, and soon the flight attendant told them to "take it outside." (At thirty-five thousand feet I thought that was a good idea to cool 'em off a bit. But I digress.) but what it really says is "unkempt bum." Guys please don't wear short, baggy shorts where your package falls out. Ladies, if you are going to wear those low-riding jeans where your thong sticks up four inches above the waistband (hip band), don't be offended when you get some crazed, animal like stares. Every time you lean forward to adjust something under the seat in front of you, all the guys will be ogling

If you want to improve the flight experience for everyone, don't wear pants that are deliberately ripped. I know this may be a fashion statement, within eyeshot will be filling their minds with images from *Hustler*. If you are that insecure that you crave all that sordid attention, then you may need more help than this book will provide. If you have nice legs, ladies, there is nothing more sensual than a short skirt to show 'em off. If you are a little uncomfortable with your weight, perhaps a muumuu may be more in line (very comfortable attire for flying).

Waist to the neck: This is where fashion for flying is perhaps most important. Some of the earlier-mentioned fashion statements can slide under the radar. But in this area of the clothed body, social awareness just has to be recognized. Perhaps one of the absolute worst is the tank top or sleeveless shirt on a man. I am getting sick just writing about it! First, you may be going to the beach or the gym or a Toby Keith concert indirectly. But the plane, full of fellow travelers, is going to drop you off first at an airport that is also full of travelers. And I don't know anybody, unless he or she has a Bigfoot fetish, who is interested in seeing, and possibly smelling, your apelike, hairy pits. Let me say it again: practice good etiquette and *put a shirt over your tank top*. Even if you are built like Mr. Universe, please wear a shirt. In fact, a rather snug shirt can show off your physique and leave a little to a woman's (or a man's) imagination. In reality, a man's body is not a work of art (just spend some time in an art museum to see what I mean). One time, there was a guy who came aboard wearing a tank top like a track star might wear. I could tell that this guy only ran from buffet to buffet.

Anyway, he had shaved his armpits. He still needed to cover up because a man shaving his armpits was disturbing in itself. Now ladies, tank tops are fine for you; it goes back to that work-of-art thing. Warning: low-cut blouses will get the high-flying wolves gawking in your direction.

Second to the tank-topped man is the donning of shirts that have socially offensive sayings on them; this applies to all sexes. Besides some of the examples mentioned earlier, some statement shirts may not be offensive to you but may stir some debate among others. It will be very rare if everyone on the plane agrees with what is stated on your shirt. For example, religious doctrine is debatable. Political opinion is debatable. Conspiracy theories are debatable. Unless your shirt states a proven fact, it is open for critique. A woman was sitting next to me with a Bible verse on her sweatshirt. I paid it no mind until she lectured me on the evils of drink (I was having my second bloody mary). Well, the hour-and-a-half flight turned into a "minicrusade," with neither one of us any wiser, holier, or drunker. Another woman, Tammy, sat next to me (I later learned her name) with a T-shirt that stated that one of the political parties was "a bunch of dumb-asses." I had to ask her why she spent money on a shirt like that. She stated that she wore it because it was true and needed to be said. I tried the "fact versus opinion" slant, but I couldn't get it through her dumb-assed head. Point being: stay away from George Carlin's "Seven Words You Can Never Say on Television" when buying a T-shirt (they still apply in today's society).

AIRPLANE ETIQUETTE

Leave sexual statements back in the bedroom (or gutter), and be ready for some conflict if a fellow passenger does not agree with what you are advertising.

Headgear: Just a few comments on hats. First, just like shirts, be mindful of what they say, especially if you find the need to wear them backward. I sat on a cross-country flight behind a guy who had a hat on backward that read "Smell my fart"…how impressive. And to all of you real cowboys and wannabe cowboys, I love a good Stetson, but they do take up valuable overhead space (I know your hat is probably worth more than most people's luggage, but it's an etiquette thing).

So, the fashion for flying is "socially conscious" for air travel. You may think you look good at your frat party or your Pilates class, but this is an airplane—a temporary societal ecosystem.

2

Packing for Security

THE SECURITY-SCREENING PROCESS can either be a series of comical errors or an inconvenience of inconsideration. The entire procedure is really quite simple and pretty efficient for a government operation. You do have an occasional TSA officer who lets the uniform go to his or her head, but for the most part, he or she is considerate and helpful. How you pack and dress before you leave home can make the process a smooth and nonembarrassing event. There are five basic removal rules to follow. If you keep these in mind when prepping to travel by air, you should breeze through security. The five rules are as follows:

1. Remove your shoes.
2. Remove you outer coat.
3. Remove your laptop from its case.

4. Remove your one-quart zip-top [per TSA] bag of liquids.
5. Remove all metals from your person

Nothing delays the process more than getting behind someone with intricate footwear. These are mainly knee-high boots that lace all the way up and require a sailor to untie and remove them. Once through the magnetometer, you have to go through the replacing process, and it is not always easy to find a place to sit down. The boots may be fashionable, but they are not practical for the security process. Another thing to keep in mind is socks. Once you remove your shoes, your feet are subject to the floor of an airport terminal. The floor is not operation-room sterile. Some airports do supply disposable footies for your screening pleasure. We can thank that guy who had explosives in his shoes for this removal rule. I say we give that guy a pair of TNT tennis shoes and tell him to "run for his life"!

Coats don't usually present too much of a problem. Pullover coats can display a little awkwardness in their removal. One time, a rather portly gentleman was attempting to remove his pullover. On the way up, he also had a hold of the shirt underneath, so they both proceeded to get stuck around his head and shoulders. He looked like an octopus trying to get out of a laundry bag. Finally, a TSA officer assisted him, and, out of breath, the gentleman continued on his way. Needless to say, many of his fellow travelers found it entertaining. Though not necessarily an etiquette issue, this story emphasizes the need to dress for ease of security.

If you travel with a laptop, just remember that it is one more thing to remove and place on the X-ray belt. One woman had hers packed in the bottom of her suitcase, requiring her to remove all of her clothes to get at it. On the other side, she basically had to repack.

And then there is the one-quart zip-top bag that was instituted when some son of a bitch tried to blow up an airplane using liquids. I don't know if that guy is still around, but I know a lot of frequent travelers who would like to stick a test tube of nitroglycerin up his ass and shake vigorously. Anyway, the rule is three ounces or less in liquids, all in a single quart-sized zip-top bag. If you are traveling for any length of time, three ounces of anything isn't going to last long. If you are checking bags, that's the best place for your liquid stuff. I still see five-ounce expensive bottles of perfume being sent to the trash. And don't forget that duty-free booze you purchased in Mexico has to be checked. And the way airline workers handle luggage, you may get home to find your clothes have had a tequila bath.

Removing metals from your person is an area that is a perennial problem. After you have removed your shoes, coat, laptop, and one-quart bag, you then remove your jewelry, watches, eyeglasses, money clips, cell phones, belts, and loose change. Invariably, you forget something, and off goes the magnetometer. You can save yourself, and everyone else, a lot of grief by taking off all of that stuff before you get to the magnetometer. I pack all of my metal in my briefcase before I even leave home. When flying, wear minimal jewelry, disconnect yourself from your cell phone for fifteen minutes (if you have the willpower), put your change in your coat pocket, and leave the rodeo belt buckle in your suitcase. I pass through airport security screening about one hundred times a year and have *never* set off the magnetometer.

So when you are packing for your airplane trip, think ahead. Ask yourself: "Am I wearing 'security-friendly' clothing? Are all my liquids three ounces or less in a one-quart zip-top bag? Have I placed all metal objects in my coat or carry-on? After I get through security, will I require a Sherpa to gather up all my junk?" If you can answer yes to the first three and no to the last, then you and your fellow travelers will have a worry-free security experience.

3

Driving at the Airport

I HAVE A HUNCH that the same people who *drive* like idiots through the airport are the same ones who *walk* like idiots through the airport (to be covered in a later chapter). During busy travel times, airports can be daunting, especially if you don't make a habit of driving through one. And of course, the bigger the airport, the more confusing, congested, and constipated it becomes. I have driven through all of the biggies, and there are three basic criteria that apply to them all:

1. Cease conversation as you enter the airport.
2. For God's sake, get off the cell phone.
3. Turn off or turn down the radio.

What do all three of these have in common? They are distractions. By discontinuing them, you will be able to focus on the business at hand. Now granted, some airport signage is sketchy at best. But at your earliest opportunity, ascertain which airline you are going to, and keep perspective on that carrier. Most airports use color coding as well, so that helps in keeping you going in the right direction. Many times, I see someone who, at the last moment, decides he or she needs to go to the red departures instead of the blue, almost causing an accident and totally oblivious to his or her movements. Horns blare and fingers fly, and all the person does is look up at signs to see if he or she is in the general vicinity. When you first arrive onto the airport property, there will be airline signs. Establish your route then, not at the zero hour. And remember, most airports have a departure level and an arrival level. The simple rule is that if you are dropping someone off to catch a flight, then that is "departures." If you are picking up, that is "arrivals." I know a lot of you are thinking, "What? Is he writing to a six-year-old?" Well, I have heard people say on their cell phones, "I am here. Where are you?" Then the next line is, "I am at *arrivals*. I just *arrived* here. Circle around, and come down one level." There is also, "I am here. Where are you?" Followed by, "Remember, I am on Delta, not US Airways." In most cases, the person who arrived by plane is in the right place. It's the person he or she is meeting who is in error.

Most airports have posted speed limits that are right up there with school zones and campgrounds. My advice is to adhere to the speed limit, as the airport police are not shy about pulling you over and issuing a citation. If you are

AIRPLANE ETIQUETTE

running late, getting pulled over just may delay your frenzied arrival.

Remember, other vehicles are using the airport as well. There are assorted hotel shuttles, car-rental shuttles, parking shuttles, taxis, limos, delivery trucks, and construction equipment. Drivers of these vehicles usually know where they are going, so if they give you a beep, it's probably because you are in the way.

The same rules apply when you are leaving the airport. Ascertain which exit you should take, and remain focused on that exit until you have completed your endeavor.

One final observation on driving through the airport: besides being focused, remain calm. There are other drivers who may be more confused than you and decide they want to be right in front of you. Before you know it, you're hitting the breaks while they are still craning their necks, looking at the signs. Just let them go, and give them a wide berth. If you have a chance, give them a copy of this book with this chapter dog-eared.

4

Curbside Unloading

HERE IS WHERE the human condition starts to fray. All of that traffic that was moving has now come to the bottleneck. And you are not only jockeying for position with other cars but with those big ol' shuttle buses as well. And they have all the grace of a three-legged hippo. Most airports will have several lanes for loading and unloading. Usually, there is one lane, sometimes two, that is *not* for stopping but for continued driving. This is usually the outside lane. However, I have seen drivers stop in the outside lane to unload passengers and their luggage and to say their good-byes. The whole time, the Hertz shuttle bus is honking its horn, only to fall on deaf ears. Would these idiots stop in a passing lane of an expressway? The answer is yes because they are inconsiderate and self-absorbed.

Now, while you are car-deep in the melee of the departure level, you need to be cognizant of not only the cars around you but also the dazed and confused people wandering about. And keep this in mind: if you are *lucky* enough to get to the inside lane and actually drop off at curbside, you will be *unlucky* enough to have to get back out to a through lane. Oh, you can put your turn signal on, but you might have better luck pushing water through a brick.

Once you do arrive at your designated airline, make the drop-off process quick and efficient. Say your long good-byes before you leave for the airport. I have seen love-struck couples saying curbside good-byes that have lasted as long as Act Two from *Romeo and Juliet*. It may be romantic, but it does not help the other three hundred people get to their planes any faster.

Also, stow your luggage so it's easy to retrieve. One time a car pulled up at O'Hare during peak departure time. It was in the third lane, which was a through lane. Both the driver and flier got out of the car. (By the way, the driver was on his cell phone.) They both wandered back and opened the trunk of the car. They had to move golf clubs, a stroller, jumper cables, a box for Goodwill, and assorted sporting equipment just to get out the guy's suitcase. Meanwhile, there were horns blowing, the driver was still on his cell phone, and there was trunk shit all over the third lane. So the flier took his suitcase and put it on the curb and then came back to help the driver repack his trunk. The driver was not much help, as he could only use one hand (his cell phone, pressed against his ear, was in the other). Eventually, the flier disappeared into the terminal. The driver opened his door, which a passing ambulance almost took off. He then drove off at ninety miles an hour, almost taking out a family of four. That guy not only needs to read this book but needs to be walloped with it!

So just to restate the curbside unloading process: say your long good-byes before you leave for the airport, have your luggage readily accessible, and get in and out quickly.

5

Ticket Counter Experience

CONGRATULATIONS, YOU HAVE finally made it inside the terminal! You are now ready to start the second leg of your travel experience. This will get you from the ticket counter to the Jetway. You will continue to practice travel etiquette, be efficient in action, and be cognizant of your fellow travelers. So with suitcase in hand, it is now time to experience the sometimes-affable ticket counter.

The first thing you will notice is an attempt to "herd the cattle." There are roped pathways to get you to the appropriate counter. The question is, which one is right for you? There is no cohesive plan when it comes to getting travelers to the ticket counter. Every airline does it differently. There can be lines for domestic coach, domestic first class and elite travelers, international coach, international business class, international first class, ticket exchanges, travelers without checked baggage, travelers needing seat assignments, and the list goes on. Basically, the more you travel, the more you become familiar with a particular airline's system. If you are not an elite flier with the airline or not first class, then you should not get in those lines (even though they are quite often shorter). Most airlines now have self-check-in kiosks. They are pretty easy to navigate, and there is usually a person nearby to assist. This is the best method if you are not checking bags or making any changes to your ticket. If you are checking bags, then get in line with the rest of the cattle, and bide your time until you get to the counter. By the way, don't put much stock in the signs above the counter. They are quite often incorrect. Some will say Open when the counters are actually closed, and vice-versa. Look at the directional signs at the start of the line to help determine your course.

When you finally get to the ticket agent or kiosk, you will need identification. *This is standard procedure at all airports* (at least the airports that you *want* to fly in and out of). A driver's license or passport is what you need. Photo identification is required. Credit cards, NRA membership cards, photos of your kids, or your library card won't get you on an airplane. Not even your birth certificate will work, because it has no photo. I was behind a gentleman who had an expired driver's license. The ticket agent let him pass, but the security TSA officer said no. So have an up-to-date photo ID. Don't leave home without it.

The ticket counter is also a good place to make seat changes and to verify flight status and departure gate information. It is not a good place to make small talk with the ticket agent. Remember, your fellow travelers would like to get on their flights as well.

The ticket counter can be a rather daunting environment, especially at an airline hub. However, this is also an area where the airlines could use some improvement in *directional signage*. Even I, an experienced traveler, can just stand and study the signs as if in a foreign land. And this even happens at airports that I frequent. So you can imagine the amateur flier's bewilderment. Some airlines place personnel near the ticket counters to assist with directions. These assistants are quite often inundated with customers and questions. I overheard one woman ask if her car would be safe in remote parking, how much would her parking would cost, and if the parking area accepted credit cards. Needless to say, after much diatribe between the two, the point was finally made that the airline employee didn't have a clue about parking matters. Another group who barely spoke English had the full attention of an employee who didn't speak Mandarin. It was a study in futility. Even the gentleman who was trying to find out what meal was being served in first class was miffed when the attendant didn't know.

So now that you know the airline employees are busy addressing more important issues, you are left to the mercy of directional signage. Those who developed most of the signage around the ticket counters either dropped out of the Ray Charles School of Transportation or they were recently promoted to highway sign director for New York City.

Basically, you have to figure out four things when checking in at the ticket counter: which airline you are traveling, destination, status of travel, and baggage intentions. Having these four things figured out will help you move from the chaos of the ticket counter to the confusion of security. Let's define the four criteria prior to bellying up to a ticket counter.

Which airline are you traveling: It sounds like it should be a no-brainer, but with mergers and code sharing, it does require some cognizance. For example, you could have a ticket issued by American Airlines, but you are actually flying on a US Airways flight code share. Or you could be flying on Alaska Airlines on a Delta ticket on a flight operated by Mesaba. (This is a combination of a merger along with a subsidiary airline operating the flight.) Most itineraries now tell you which air carrier to check in with. Be advised: if you are traveling on one airline but have been ticketed on another and there is an interruption in travel, you will need to rebook, and be prepared for a battle of responsibility.

Destination: Not so much which city but rather domestic or international. Make sure you are in the proper line. Flying to Rome, Georgia, won't do you any good if you are in the line for Rome, Italy. It is especially good to know where you are going if you are checking luggage. Case in point: I was traveling to Detroit, Michigan (airport code DTW). When the airline agent handed me my baggage claim ticket, she said, "One bag checked to Dallas" (airport code DFW).

AIRPLANE ETIQUETTE

If I hadn't been paying attention, it would have been a same-outfit-two-days-in-a-row situation.

Status of travel: If you are an elite traveler booked in first or business class, there are usually designated ticket counter areas for you. If you are in coach, then stand in the appropriate line. I know the line is usually longer, but there are a greater number of travelers using that class of service. Most airlines have expedited lanes for travelers not checking bags or making travel changes.

Baggage intentions: Again, there are usually designated lines for travelers who want to check bags. If you don't plan on checking bags, avoid these lines, as they can move a little slower. If you are checking luggage, there are four rules I recommend following:

1. Have luggage identification on the suitcase before you get to the counter.
2. Remove all straps.
3. Don't check valuables or breakables.
4. Don't overpack.

If you take the time to fill out and attach a luggage-identification tag while you are standing at the counter, you are not practicing good etiquette. You are delaying your fellow travelers. All external straps should come off, as they can get caught in the mechanized baggage handlers, and this would also cause a delay. You are asking for trouble if you pack valuables or breakables. Lost luggage is most often found, but the gorillas handling the luggage could present a problem for fragile items. If you have ever seen how baggage is moved around the airport, you will understand how items can come up "broken." On an international flight, a friend of mine's luggage was mishandled, and he did not notice it for three weeks. Needless to say, the gold-and-emerald crucifix that had been in his family for three generations and had been carefully packed between his socks was missing. So many people and places had touched that bag, it was nearly impossible to track down. Another time, a woman had packed a jar of homemade pickled beets in her suitcase carefully, or so she thought. When she retrieved her bag in Chicago…well, let's say she basically threw out the purple-soaked suitcase.

So, you have survived the ticket counter experience. Now it's time to move on to the next bottleneck: the security-screening process.

6

Moving Through Security

This is where the bottleneck gets a little tighter. This is also where a little preplanning can go a long way. Once again, you will need to determine the proper line. There is usually one dedicated to frequent fliers and/or first class. There may also be a designated line for airline personnel. Then there is the line (usually the longest) for the casual flier. The first sentry will check your boarding pass and picture ID. Driver's licenses and/or passports are the best (neither of which should be expired). The agent will verify that you are indeed flying on that day and that you are heading to the correct gate. He or she may also make a split-second decision to have extra security directed your way and may scribble things on your boarding pass, most of which may as well be hieroglyphics. However, there is one thing that will catch the next TSA agent's attention, which may cause you to get additional screening: complaining about the process. After you pass through Checkpoint Charlie, you will have to determine what the best lane for moving through the magnetometer or body scanner is. I suggest avoiding lanes with children, people who may not understand English, anybody talking on cell phones, or people with a lot of stuff. To stay clear of all four is a red-letter day and should be cause for an overall good feeling. If you fly a lot, then TSA Precheck is the way to go—less amateur travelers and an overall quicker experience (or it should be).

As you approach the sterile-looking tables where you will unload, keep in mind that this is where the suggestions in chapter two are going to be appreciated. Remember that all footwear must be removed, as well as outer garments such as coats, sports coats, etc. Most jewelry can actually stay on with the exception of watches, big belt buckles, and excessive bling. You will also need to place your laptop in a bin and your one-quart bag of liquid items (three ounces or less per item). One thing that does not go on the X-ray belt is your boarding pass. Keep that in your hand.

You are now at the stainless-steel table that funnels into the X-ray machine. One final check: shoes, one-quart bag of liquid items, electronics, outer garments, metal items—all in a plastic bin. The only items you should have left are basic clothing, a boarding pass, and a little dignity. I recommend staying with your personal items until they are on the conveyer belt and bound for the tunnel. Next, you will patiently wait until the TSA agent motions you through the magnetometer. If there is no beep, you may continue to retrieve your stuff, which will be out of the tunnel shortly. If you set off an alarm, you *will* be noticed, not only by the TSA but by your fellow travelers as well. The agents will ask you to double-check for metal items, and then they will ask you to pass through again. Another alarm and you get to go for additional screening mano a mano. Be cool, and just follow their instructions. If one of your items is selected for additional screening, just let it go. Don't question or fight it. You aren't going to win. A rather well-dressed businessman's carry-on was visually inspected by an agent. The whole time the agent was looking through the stuff, the man was complaining about how the agent was handling his items. When the traveler reached out and grabbed the agent's wrist in an attempt to control the situation, things turned interesting. Three additional agents appeared, and an officer of the law (packing heat) converged on the scene. Needless to say, the disgruntled man spent some additional time in a security office while things were sorted out. Just before the door of the airplane was closed, he scooted in and sat right next to me (my lucky day). He rambled on, to anyone who would listen, about his trials at security. When he asked me what I thought about his story, I simply responded that he wasn't going to win. Not the sympathy he was looking for.

After you start to gather you belongings at the end of the tunnel, keep in mind that there are fellow travelers *right* behind you. Grab all your stuff, and *move along to get out of the way*! Get it? Get your life back in order away from the X-ray machine. Granted, there are not always ample "redressing" areas. But standing at the secure side of the X-ray machine is *not* a good place to reassemble. This is basically a drain into the airport. If you are putting your stuff back in its proper place at the X-ray table, then you are in fact blocking the drain. To reiterate: the less you have to place on the conveyer belt, the quicker you will be able to pass through the drain. Of course, you also have the option of bypassing the magnetometer and body scanner and opting for a pat down.

7

Moving Through the Airport

Moving through an airport is not much different than driving down a US highway. Stay to the right-hand side of the passageway. If you are moving slowly, stay way right, allowing faster-moving travelers to pass you on the left. If you need to get to the opposite side of the aisle, plan your movement through the oncoming crowd, keeping in mind that there are people behind you, next to you, and in front of you, just like driving. If you are in a group moving en masse, don't take up the entire walkway. Walk in a column until you reach your destination, and then regroup for conversation. There is also the observation that people who talk on cell phones while driving usually drive like shit. The same is true with people who try to walk and talk at the same time. They are oblivious. The ones who try texting while walking are even worse. They obviously can't multitask, and that inability is detrimental to moving through the airport. If you have to talk or text, *pull over*! Get out of the active runway (so to speak).

Here is another faux pas: stopping in the *middle* of the passageway to have a conversation! Intellect has it that these talkers would notice that they are in the way. But they are wrapped up in their own little worlds. You could walk by dragging a twenty-foot anaconda, and they wouldn't even notice. It has taken a lot of willpower not to body block them into the linoleum. The other irksome sort is the person who is moving along with the flow of traffic and all of a sudden comes to a dead stop…why? One time in the San Antonio airport, a cowboy was tailgating a woman when, all of a sudden, she hit the brakes. Well, old Tex couldn't make the adjustment and plowed right into her. Cowboy hats and carry-ons went flying as the woman fell to her knees with the perpetrator straddling her. In hindsight, it was Texas. I suppose they could have been practicing for the rodeo.

As far as those moving walkways go, many people ignore proper procedure. Announcements and signage will instruct you to *stand* on the right to allow passengers to *pass* on the left, similar to driving in the United States. I quit using the moving walkways because it was always a crapshoot of whom I would be moving along with. It's very simple: stand on the right, and walk on the left. If you are traveling with somebody, don't stand next to each other. If you are standing and

AIRPLANE ETIQUETTE

decide you want to walk, look before you step into the fast lane. I have seen collisions of huge magnitude. And for those of you who are moving quickly, *watch your luggage*! Those moving walkways are usually narrow, so be cognizant of your briefcase, purse, carry-on, backpack, and roller board. You have to position such items directly in front of you or behind you when passing on the moving walkway. Note: if you choose to stand on the walkway, cell-phone usage is permitted. Just get it together when the walkway ends, or you may end up facedown with a broken phone. And remember, the moving walkway is *not* a toy for your undisciplined kids to play on. Not only do they get in the way, but they actually may get maimed if they get their fingers in the grate mechanism. One time in the Norfolk airport, a mom was talking on her cell phone, oblivious, while little junior was playing on the moving walkway. He didn't get his fingers stuck, but his untied shoelace ended up getting caught in the grate. He didn't get hurt, but it sure scared the hell out of the little guy. Of course, the mom was pissed at the airport.

Some airports like Atlanta and Denver use an internal monorail-type system to move people around. So when the monorail doors are open and you are more than five feet away and you hear "the doors are closing," don't make another move. Don't try to beat the doors from closing. You wouldn't try to beat a train, would you? Anyway, attempting to rush aboard just before the door closes is a selfish inconsideration to your fellow passengers. What invariably happens is you or your suitcase interferes with the closing mechanism, and the doors reopen. You may feel that you have a little victory, but now the doors are back open for other morons to try and sneak on. I have actually been on a tram when five people cheated the system and caused a temporary shutdown. All of the travelers were delayed because one individual couldn't wait five minutes. So show some etiquette, and don't try to beat the door. If you need some kind of menial accomplishment, try dodging traffic.

When you are moving through the airport, restrooms, concessions, eateries, trams, or just about any public space, keep in mind that if you are toting luggage, your personal space has just expanded. Instead of taking up four square feet, you may now be occupying as much as twelve square feet! Be aware of your environmental positioning, and try not to knock others on their asses.

8

Boarding Areas

So now you have maneuvered your way through the airport and have arrived at the boarding area. The first thing you may notice is a lack of waiting space. This is especially true in older airports like New York LaGuardia and Chicago Midway. On average, a 737 aircraft will accommodate 150 people. Most boarding areas fall well short of that. So you may find yourself standing or even waiting in an adjacent boarding area. If you are lucky enough to claim a seat, here are some etiquette guidelines to follow.

The chair next to you is not a luggage holder. Place your luggage on the floor. A fellow passenger may want to use the seat for its intended purpose. And when placing your luggage on the floor, be cognizant of its location. There is usually not a lot of walking space in the boarding area, so make sure someone won't accidentally trip over your junk unless you are looking for one of those waste-of-taxpayer-money, dumb-ass, self-absorbed, I'm-worthless lawsuits. Don't get me started on that subject! Anyway, don't treat your seat as if it were a recliner. I can't tell you how many times I have to step over someone's stretched-out legs. And of course, that person makes no attempt to pull them in. One time I stepped over someone's legs but forgot about the suitcase I was pulling and proceeded to drag it over his legs. A few disgusted remarks later (by both of us), and the individual got the message that he was not alone in the boarding area.

Consider your environment (the people around you). If you plan on having a meaningless conversation on your cell phone (and most of them are meaningless to everyone except the talker), keep your voice down. Really, no one cares about your Uncle Max's gallbladder, your inept coworker, or how much you miss your "smoochie." And that stinky Mediterranean goulash sandwich you are munching on may be tasty to you, but it may have your fellow passengers dry heaving in their laps. Just eat your lunch in a more personal area.

If you arrive before the gate agent does (and this is usually the case), don't rush to the check-in counter as soon as he or she arrives. The agents have to get organized, reboot the computer, talk on the phone to Larry in baggage, check their cell-phone messages, type a bunch of who-knows-what on the keyboard, and make several trips to the Jetway. Once they have accomplished all of those tasks, you can approach them. Take my advice—if you try to interact with them too soon, you won't get your seat changed or information verified. I always wait for someone else to go up and break the ice (so to speak).

And be aware that there are quite often seats that are designated for the elderly and/or handicapped. If you do not meet either of these criteria, keep moving. These are not the seats you are looking for. Note: being a selfish idiot does not qualify as being mentally handicapped. Also, if you are hungover or tired and feel like 110, that does not qualify you either.

If you have children with you, please watch them carefully. Some airports actually provide play areas. These are perfect places to wait with children. But if you are in the boarding area with fellow passengers, remind your kids that they are not at home. Tell them not to jump or climb on the seats. Tell them not to play in the aisleways. Tell them not to touch people or their personal items with their grubby little fingers. And make sure they don't cough or sneeze near anybody. Keep your precious little petri dishes in quarantine.

Here is another environmental consideration to keep in mind. I have had the unfortunate experience of sitting next to a woman who decided to change her baby's diaper *right there in the boarding area*! The baby must have eaten a stewed aardvark, because, well...I won't go into details. Let's just say that diaper cleared a room quicker than a leper at the buffet. I know babies don't poop on a schedule. But all you have to do is take your stinky-ass kid to a bathroom. They are equipped to handle such predicaments.

So now that you have mastered the boarding area, the gate agent will soon announce, "Flight 247 to Rapid City will soon be ready for general boarding." Don't move yet…

9

Boarding the Aircraft

WHEN IT COMES to boarding an aircraft, the airlines like to use the old hurry-up-and-wait routine. They make an announcement to state that they will be making an announcement to board the aircraft. All this really does is create mild panic among the passengers, and it makes them worry that if they don't get to the Jetway, they will miss the flight. Not true. If you follow the directives of the airline, you will get on in plenty of time. But the key word is "follow." With the exception of Southwest Airlines and perhaps some other carriers, you will be assigned a seat. In order for the process to move smoothly, you need to board when your seating area is called. Most airlines use a zone system in the boarding process. Your zone is usually printed right below your seat assignment on your boarding pass. Again, do not attempt to board the plane until your zone number has been announced. Here is how the process is supposed to work.

First, airlines will usually board wheelchairs and people who need a little extra time down the Jet way (travelers with small children). Clear the path, and let these people through. Second, first/business class will be called. (Sometimes, they will board the exit rows at this time too.) Third, members of the frequent flier program will start moving. If you are not in any of these preliminary groups, *move your sorry ass out of the way*! You are blocking the flow of traffic. On occasion, I have seen passengers in zone five try to board in zone one. The gate agents actually have pulled these people aside and made them wait, under the smirking eyes of their fellow passengers.

There is a theory that the sooner you get on an airplane, the better overhead space is available. That is actually a fact. These days, the last ones on usually have to gate check their stuff. Now, this little problem has been brought on by the airlines. By charging ridiculous prices for checking luggage, most travelers try to use carry-ons. The rule is one carry-on to fit in the overhead bin or under the seat in front of you and a personal item such as a small purse or briefcase. I have seen suitcases the size of Dumbo get on a plane and travelers carrying on three pieces of luggage. These people are nothing less than rude and inconsiderate.

As you approach the agent scanning the tickets, take a break from your meaningless cell-phone conversation and acknowledge the individual who is allowing you access to the airplane. That's just common courtesy.

AIRPLANE ETIQUETTE

As mentioned in the previous chapter, some of the older airports don't have adequate boarding areas. So what happens is that as people start to line up for their anticipated zone to be called, they spill out into an active walkway, and as usual, they are oblivious to the fact that no one can get by them. They are dead set on boarding that aircraft. Figure it out. If you were walking down the hallway on *your* way to *your* flight, wouldn't you want access to get to *your* boarding area? It goes back to environmental awareness. Take notice of how your actions are affecting other people.

Once again, it all comes down to environmental awareness and *listening* to the gate agents' instructions. If everyone boarded according to plan, you would be surprised at how much less stress there would be and how much easier it would be to have an on-time departure.

10

Gate Checking

GATE CHECKING USUALLY happens one of three ways:

1. You manage to get your behemoth past security, but the gate agent says that it is too big.
2. You are on the airplane, and, low and behold, all of the overhead bins are full because nobody wants to pay to check bags and most people are bin hogs.
3. It is a regional or commuter jet that has limited storage space.

If you manage to get past the scrutinizing eyes of the TSA, you still have to pass the gate-agent gauntlet. I have seen people board the aircraft with suitcases the size of Delaware. Talk about bin hogs! Not to mention that their other "small carry-on" is the size of the Titanic. They must have used the old Jedi mind trick: "These are not the bags you are looking for."

Lately, I have seen more gate agents pull the trigger on these cargo haulers. If an agent singles you out and asks you to gate check, consider it as somewhat of a bonus. You now can travel lighter without the additional fees of checking. Even if you are not keen on the idea, you aren't going to win. The agent is the sheriff of boarding areas. I overheard one gentleman tell the gate agent that he just couldn't gate check his minivan of a suitcase because all of his prescriptions were in it. Either he had more diseases than a leper colony, or he had half of Colombia in there, if you know what I mean.

It is the same situation if you have already boarded. Consider it an economical bonus to gate check. The worst thing you can do is get all pissed off and try and schlep your Winnebago to the front of the aircraft. There is not a lot of room for people to get out of the way. If you try to go "upstream," bitching all the while, you will just bring your fellow passengers down to your pitiful level. Just wait for the oncoming passengers to get seated, and then bring your suitcase to the front for checking. Then go back to your seat, sit down, and be quiet!

On commuter flights or regional aircraft, there is quite often just enough space for a briefcase. For your suitcase, you will get a gate claim ticket, and one will be attached to your suitcase. You will then leave your bag at a designated area in the Jetway. Board the airplane and relax. When you get to your destination, you will claim your bag, somewhere

AIRPLANE ETIQUETTE

in the same vicinity where you dropped it (obviously in a different airport...hopefully). If you are instructed to claim it on the jet way, stand to one side so others may pass. Sounds like simple instructions, right? The key words are *stand*, *one side*, and *pass*.

Stand means don't sit or squat or roam around on your cell phone. *One side* means everybody stands on the same *one* side. When both sides of the Jetway are lined up with stiffs, the final word, *pass*, is not going to happen. The rules are simple: Give the ramp crew ample space to place the bags. Don't crowd the access door. Stand on one side. The first passenger there will usually determine what side you stand on. When you see your suitcase, grab it, and get the hell out of the way. Do all of your adjustments outside the jet way. If you have children, keep them close at hand. Get strollers out of the way as well. The Jetway is an active walkway just like the terminal.

When you remove the claim check from your suitcase, don't just throw it on the floor (you are not home). That is considered littering and poor etiquette, and in some countries, you will hang for it!

11

Moving Through the Aircraft

THIS IS WHERE I sit in my seat and shake my head in disgust. Even after being on thousands of flights, I still marvel at how dysfunctional human beings can be. The action is moving down a one-way aisle to a designated destination. Doesn't that sound fairly simple? It's a part of everyday life, moving from point A to point B. It's the brain telling the feet where to move. But I'm afraid that Sigmund Freud and Albert Einstein would have a field day watching the mind try to navigate the physics of an airplane aisle. Words like "incompetent," "inconsiderate," and "unaware" come to mind. Let me tell you first how it really should go down. Then I will tell the horror stories of how it unfortunately happens.

When you first enter the aircraft, you will be greeted by a flight attendant or maybe even a law enforcement officer. If he or she acknowledges you, be courteous and respond. Even a smile will suffice. I *strongly* suggest that you not talk or text on your cell phone, play your Game Boy, listen to your iPod, or, God forbid, work on your computer or tablet when walking to your seat. Most of you can't multitask...no really, *you can't*. So keep to the issue at hand, which is efficiently getting to your seat. As you walk down the very narrow aisle, you need to be extra cognizant of what you are carrying. If you are juggling too much stuff, you need to deplane and take a bus. A suitcase, carry-on, jacket, cell phone, and Starbucks are *way* too much stuff. If you are pulling a roller board, you need to adjust your body so that when you are dragging it, it does not get hung up on seats or people's feet. If you have a shoulder bag, you need to dislodge it from your shoulder and carry it directly in front of you. I can't emphasize this one enough. If I had a dollar for every time I got banged by somebody's inconsideration, well, then I wouldn't have to write this book for a living. If you keep the carry-on on your shoulder, it becomes wider than the aisle, and you proceed to whack people in the head or shoulder. Most times, the perpetrators are so oblivious that there is no mention of an apology. As you are walking down the aisle, keep your seat number in mind. If you're assigned seat is 8A and you go all the way back to 18A and say, "oops," then you just need to step out of the aisle and wait for an opportunity to go back "upstream." Anyway, as you near your seat, start scoping out

AIRPLANE ETIQUETTE

overhead space for your luggage. Simply stow your bag, and sit down. If you need to retrieve something out of your bag, kindly step out of the aisle so others may pass. If you have an assigned seat, take it. Don't take someone else's seat on the chance he or she won't mind. Take your seat, and negotiate after the plane has boarded. And don't bother the flight attendants with your trivial needs. They have more important matters other than where to seat you.

So that is how it is supposed to happen: stay focused on your destination, be aware of your fellow passengers, and move along!

Here's the bitter truth.

The absolute worst, the three-headed monster, is the passenger who is on a cell phone and has an overpacked shoulder bag and a grande latte. This is the poster child for selfishness. This is the reason for birth control. This is a person who never brings anything to a party, stands up during a play at a football game, and drives slowly in the passing lane. And I am here to tell you, someone like this is on just about every flight.

Another problem child is the one who eludes both security and the gate agent when it comes down to luggage size. So now this individual is on the plane, trying to stuff a blimp into the overhead. It's an old physics theory (I think). You can't fit five pounds of stuff into a three-pound bag (or something like that). So while the entire boarding process is on hold, this individual is trying to slam his or her suitcase into the overhead. All the time saying things like, "I did not have this problem on my last flight," or, "Are these abnormally small bins?" It's possible that you may have had larger bins on your last flight, but it's more probable that you are just an inconsiderate bonehead. Usually, the result is turning the passenger's suitcase sideways, thus hogging three-quarters of the bin. But at least he or she is out of the aisle and progress starts back up.

Another one that is irksome is the individual who stows luggage and then proceeds to remove his or her Tom Clancy book, iPod, neck pillow, and laptop. Did I mention it was on a forty-minute flight? What a boob! The Tom Clancy book alone is a transpacific flight.

So keep in mind when moving through an airplane that it is a narrow one-way road. It just switches directions when deplaning. And that on either side of the aisle are human bodies that bruise easily.

12

Stowing Luggage

STOWING LUGGAGE ON an airplane is quite often a comedy of errors. This section alone could probably fill an entire book. Of course, the airlines didn't help any when they imposed a checked-baggage fee. Now, in order to save money, travelers try and fit three weeks of stuff into a carry-on.

The first rule of luggage stowage is as follows: keep your belongings near your seat. I have seen many passengers come aboard, take the first open bins for their valises, and then go back twenty rows to their seats. That type of inconsideration only causes a ripple effect when passengers with up-front seating arrive to find the overhead bins above their seats occupied. They move farther down the aisle till they find space. And guess what? It's right over the seat of the passengers whose stuff is up front! Then the up-front passengers have to move upstream to get back to their assigned seats, and now a whole bunch of people are perturbed.

The second rule of luggage stowage is as follows: if you can't lift it into the bin, check it. I have been called upon to help lift steamer trunks into the overhead space. I used to accommodate these passengers, but not anymore. I am not a porter. One time a young woman asked for my assistance. She claimed she had carpal tunnel and couldn't lift anything. Not only did she have ninety pounds of cement in her bag, but it was overstuffed and wouldn't fit into the bin. When I turned to let her know it was a no-go, she was five rows back in her seat. Meanwhile, I was holding up the boarding process. I informed her of the situation, and she asked if I could take it up front and have the flight attendant check it. I told her that my gate-check fee was thirty-five dollars. She should check next time and save ten dollars. Needless to say, she was not amused. But then again, neither was I. By the way, the flight attendants have more important things to do than helping a passenger with an overstuffed bag. Either pack lighter or check it at the ticket counter.

The third rule of luggage stowage is as follows: don't be a bin hog. You should only be toting two items—a suitcase and a briefcase or purse-type thing. And there is a good chance that both are bulging at the seams. So put one of the items in the overhead space and the other under the seat in front of you. That is *in front* of you. The space *under* your seat actually belongs to the passenger behind you. (The exception to this rule is if you are seated in a bulkhead row or exit row.) The item that is under the seat in front of you cannot stick out into the area where the window-seated person has to walk. If someone trips over your stuff in an emergency and ends up dying, won't you be riddled with guilt? For all of you people with guitars, fishing poles, display tubes, sombreros, or any other oddly shaped items, please be aware of the bin space you are hoarding. Those items tend to take up some square footage, and not in a symmetrical manner. Ask a flight attendant if there is room in a forward closet.

The fourth rule of luggage stowage is as follows: the bins were designed to be closed in a civil manner. If you have to slam the bin several times to get it to latch, then your suitcase has got to go. I have been on flights where the bins have been abused one too many times, and they no longer latch. Guess what? This causes a flight delay so maintenance persons can get their slow-moving asses on board to repair the bin. I have also been on flights where the bins have popped open during flight and have actually seen coats and things fall out onto someone's unsuspecting head. Don't be a jackass. If it does not fit or if the bin door does not close easily, check it.

The fifth rule of luggage stowage is as follows: get the stuff you want out of your bag before you stow it and get to your seat. Another inconsiderate and selfish display is placing your luggage in the bin, and then, while still standing in an active aisle, taking inventory of what you may need for the flight. If you are talking on a cell phone while doing this, you probably have deep-rooted emotional issues. If you are talking on a cell phone *and* juggling a cup of Starbucks, well, then you are just class A inconsiderate.

There are a couple of other important issues regarding stowing luggage. Don't place breakables in the overhead and expect your fellow travelers to notice. They will get broken. It's best to keep those under the seat in front of you. If your bag is too large for under the seat, see if you can get some blankets to pack around it in the bin. And don't put your fresh catch or anything else that stinks in the bins. I have actually had this happen. The two-and-a-half-hour flight smelled like a cannery on a hot August day. Ship those types of perishables next-day air (on a cargo plane).

The overhead bins, just like the rest of the places on your journey, are a shared space. Have some consideration for your fellow travelers who also need a little room.

13

The Preflight Lecture

So now, we have all been cattle driven to our seats, and the boarding door has been closed. An announcement will be forthcoming stating that the forward door has been closed and to please turn off all electronic devices, including cell phones. Apparently, every flight has its fair share of people who are hard of hearing, or they figure the rules do not apply to them. The ones who really get me are the cellphone users who, after being told by the flight attendant to turn off their phones, hang up and make another call. The flight attendants meant for them to turn the power off on their phones, not just end their conversations. The real insignificant jerk is the one who has his or her cell phone on loud ring and answers it while the plane is barreling down the runway approaching lift-off speed. I once asked a guy sitting next to me if that was the Mayo Clinic calling about his liver transplant. He didn't get it. I told him that the only call that was important enough to answer during takeoff would have to be something along those lines. Of course, he was the same dipstick whose phone began ringing on landing approach. He must have been really important…at least in his own remedial mind. He tried to authenticate his viability by telling me that cell phones don't really interfere with cockpit communications. I asked him what he did for a living. He was an investment broker. I asked him how a person who gambles with other people's money for a living had any expertise in the field of communications or, for that matter, FAA operations. His intelligent retort was a repeat of how cell phones don't really interfere with communications. I said that they sure do when you are talking at forty decibels above the rest of the plane and when everyone can hear you. Not to mention, *nobody cares about your conversation.*

So my point here is *turn off that ridiculous cell phone!*

The next level of rudeness comes from people who carry on *loud* conversations when the flight attendants are delivering their safety instructions and are asking for your attention. This is especially apparent in first class. Now I have flown enough times on enough different aircrafts that I could easily deliver the speech. That does not give me the right to talk over it. There actually may be people on board who are not familiar with the safety spiel, or perhaps they find some solace in hearing it. Whatever the reason, kindly cease your meaningless conversation for approximately three minutes. Look out the window, suck your thumb, or just close your

AIRPLANE ETIQUETTE

eyes and visualize that you are considerate. If an emergency ever did occur and one of you loudmouths got in my way to an emergency exit because you did not really know what to do...well, it may not turn out pleasant.

If you are seated in an exit row, please be sure you are up to the task if there is an emergency. If there is, you will have to reach way down inside yourself and find the inner strength to carry out the task. It's not like on TV. The exit row is also not just for extra legroom. There is some potential responsibility that goes along with those seats. Unfortunately, I have seen ninety-year-old feeble women and non-English-speaking travelers—and even a person with a cast on one arm—all sitting at various times in the exit row. Sometimes even the flight attendants get a little preoccupied and overlook some rules.

So basically for preflight, keep your mouth shut for the safety debriefing and be honestly prepared to handle the exit-row responsibilities. Now, we are finally in the air.

14

The In-Flight Experience

THE WHEELS HAVE left the ground, and the plane is starting its climb to cruising altitude. At this point, the Fasten Seat Belt sign is still illuminated. This means *stay in your seat*! The item that you think you desperately need in the overhead bin will have to wait until the captain says so. On several occasions, I have seen passengers stand up a mere five hundred feet off the ground and open the overhead bin in search of some inconsequential item. One time a bin popped open, and a briefcase fell out onto an unsuspecting passenger. The plane was at a pretty good angle at that time, so items were not level in the bins. This point in the flight is also a prime time to lose one's balance and fall on one's dumb ass, or worse, an innocent victim. Wait until the captain turns off the Fasten Seat Belt sign before you get up and wander around the cabin.

So now you are at cruising altitude, and the seat-belt sign is off. Bear in mind that if there is turbulence or rough weather, the sign will stay illuminated. During these particular times, it is very important to stay seated. If the captain asks the flight attendants to stay seated and they are professionals, then you amateurs better keep your asses in your seats. But if all is clear and the seat-belt sign is off, then you may now visit the overhead bins and lavatories. It is *not* an opportunity to stand in the aisleway and loiter. There is a good chance that the flight attendants will be moving through the aisles with service carts, and they certainly don't want to have to maneuver around you.

On the subject of lavatories, there are a couple of etiquette rules that apply. If the flight has several classes of service and the flight attendants have requested that you use the lavatories in your class, then please adhere to the request. Quite often, the forward lavatory is near the cockpit, and the airlines do not want a gathering of ninnies with full bladders lurking around the flight-deck door. This is a security issue. When you are done with the facilities, please be considerate of the next person in line: flush, throw away any paper, and clean up after yourself. If that three-bean and jalapeno burrito decides it wants an exit strategy at thirty thousand feet, well, do what you can to clear the air for the next passenger.

Another thing to keep in mind is that the flight attendants are not your personal valets, nor are they waitstaff. They are providing a service to you by offering a beverage

AIRPLANE ETIQUETTE

and maybe some sort of basic snack, but their primary function is your safety. On one flight, the passenger next to me asked if I would flag down the "waitress" because he needed another gin and tonic. I didn't, but she overheard him. No more gin and tonics for the swine.

If you are seated in an aisle seat and plan on sleeping, remember that the other passengers next to you may have to wake you up to get to the aisle. Don't be a defensive dork. They have all the right in the world to get up and say "excuse me" on their way out. Now, if they don't say "excuse me," go ahead and trip them on their way by—wait, no, that would be poor etiquette.

Another issue I have with some sleepers on airplanes is that they snore like a buffalo. Maybe they should try sleeping face down on their tray tables. On one flight, a rather attractive woman next to me nodded off. I woke her up after she had saturated my upper arm with drool.

15

Final Approach

Now the pinnacle of your trip has passed, and you are about to touch down at your destination (hopefully). At some point, the pilot will turn on the Fasten Seat Belt sign for the duration of the flight. This always seems to be an indication to get up and go to the lavatory. For all those dyslexic dingdongs, it means the opposite—stay in your seat for landing! An announcement will also be made to power down all electronic devices. The key word here is *all*. This is also the time to finish your beverage. The flight attendants will be by to pick up your trash, including your beverage cup. You can also pass along newspapers and other flotsam you have accumulated. This will assist the cleaners and possibly speed up the turnaround time on the flight. The flight attendants are not really fond of getting disgusting things like gum or snotty tissues, but then again, leaving them in the seat pocket is pretty Neanderthalian as well. You will also be asked to raise tray tables and seat backs. This is for safety in case a speedy exit is needed. I have seen passengers recline their seats fully after they have been told to raise them for landing. Now, if I have to exit my row quickly, I will have to navigate past the reclined seat back. I have already determined that if needed, I will simply go over the seat.

It's not uncommon at certain altitudes to hear cell-phone beeps, rings, and whirs. Either a few bozos forgot to turn their phones off or they are a little premature in turning them back on. It's one thing to have your phone ring and act all innocent and surprised. It's another to actually answer it while the plane is still on approach. What a dung brain! I actually heard someone's phone ring at about a thousand feet. I heard the person answer it and say, "I can't talk right now. We haven't landed yet." *What?* Hey, here is an idea: *don't answer the phone*! Better yet, turn it off.

So now, the plane has landed. It's time for all of the idiot juices to rise to the surface again. All you trigger-happy assholes with your fingers on your cell phones can *now* turn them on and tell the persons on the other end that you have just landed and will call them when you get to the gate… which, under normal circumstances, will be in about fifteen minutes. I love this one. "What's the weather like?" How about looking out the window, you bowling ball? Then when you get to the gate, you call and say, "I am at the gate. I will call you when I get off the plane…how was the movie

AIRPLANE ETIQUETTE

last night?" And yes, when you get off the plane, it's, "I just stepped off the plane. I'll call you from baggage claim...no, wait. I'll meet you at baggage claim...read any good books lately?"

I am not exaggerating...I have heard meaningless conversations just like those.

Anyway, as the plane is taxiing to the gate, you must still remain seated. The captain, who is in charge, will let you know when to arise by turning off the seat-belt sign. This is a terrible time to stand up and open up the overheads. (Oh, I have seen it done dozens of times.) Sometimes the idiots fall on someone else. Sometimes items from the open bin fall on somebody else. Usually, the results are not positive. This practice is especially apparent when the flight is late and travelers are making tight connections. They figure by retrieving their overhead junk early, they can get a jump on exiting. *Never works!* One time, there were some soldiers in the back of the plane. They were coming home after a tour in Iraq. The plane was late, and they had very tight connections. The flight attendant asked if everyone would stay seated and allow the servers of our country to retrieve their gear and exit first. There were about a dozen passengers who either were deaf, inconsiderate selfish pricks, or un-American communists. They stood up, got their stuff, and tried to ace the servicemen off the plane. I hope they appreciate their freedoms.

16

The Disembarking Process

IF YOU WANT to witness the complete breakdown of the human condition, just watch passengers attempt to get off of an airplane. In theory, it would seem to be a simple process, since it is basically a one-way route of exit. But people are selfish, ignorant, distracted, lazy, rushed, and mainly discourteous. On paper, here is how the disembarkation process should play out.

First, no one should make a move until the captain has turned off the seat-belt sign. You self-absorbed people who try to get a jump on the system are the ones who start the unraveling process. After the seat-belt sign is turned off, the aisle-seated passengers should be the only ones standing in the aisle. Do not try to clear an entire row of seats into the aisle. It is physically impossible. That is why airlines board the way they do. Anyway, now that the aisle-seated passengers are up, they can open the overhead bins *carefully*. Items do shift (as the flight attendants point out), and when the bin door is flung open, Mr. Businessman's computer case could fall out on Little Johnny's cranium. Now the aisle-seated passengers can retrieve their belongings. All the passengers in row one are the first to leave unless they signal to move on. Then row two, row three, and row four…get the picture? The aisle-seated passengers go first, followed by center seat, and the window seat is last. For example, if you are seated in row twenty-one, you will wait for row twenty to clear, and then you will exit, followed by your fellow passengers in row twenty-one. This is basically an act of courtesy. It may be the only one you practice that day (or ever), but that is how it is done. On double-aisle aircrafts where you have both aisles meeting at the door of the plane to exit, the proper etiquette is every other passenger (or travel group), much like a four-way stop. Of course, if you are oblivious at four-way stops, then you may have trouble handling the multiexit of an aircraft. Once it is your turn to gather your stuff, don't try to do it while juggling that cell-phone call. Cease your meaningless conversation until you are well inside the terminal. If you have kids, sure it's cute that they have their own Mickey Mouse roller boards and blankies. But it may not be cute to the one hundred passengers still behind you. Hurry Little Timmy along or carry him unless you already have eight things you are juggling, in which case you need to go back to the beginning of this book.

AIRPLANE ETIQUETTE

If you are one of those unfortunate passengers who is seated five or six rows ahead of your luggage, you have several options: ask if someone would be kind enough to pass your suitcase forward to you; wait until someone further back is clogging up the process, and then make a bold move upstream; or wait until all passengers have deplaned. Trying to weasel by people who are leaving in the proper manner is *not* an option. If you have a traveling companion and you temporarily get separated by fellow passengers, don't be frightened. You will be reunited in a few minutes.

When you are removing your junk from the overheads, please be cognizant of the many people around you. Don't try to don your jacket. You may end up punching somebody or throwing an errant elbow. When you bring your valise down to the aisle, again, don't inadvertently knock someone in the head, and don't set it on someone's foot. I bring these up because they have all happened to me...more than once.

If you want to go beyond the call of niceness, hand the person sitting next to you his or her luggage. But the passenger should still be sitting, not standing in the aisle, because you have not vacated that spot yet.

Now that you have exited the aircraft, you are walking up the jet way. This is *not* the time to stop and get yourself organized. I know it is a little wider than the airplane aisle, but it is still an active runway for passengers. Once inside the terminal, there will be ample space to get your act together (if possible). On regional jets where you have to wait for your gate-checked luggage to be sent to the Jetway, everybody waiting should stand on the same one side. In other words, get your lame ass out of the center of the Jetway! Not all travelers have to wait for their American Touristers, and they would just like to move along. Also, don't stand right in front of the door where workers bring in the luggage. With your brontosaurus butt in the way, the ground personnel can't bring in the bags. *Step aside!* And once you get your suitcase, get moving. Go to the terminal, and get organized.

So use a little thought process when getting off an airplane. Be courteous to your fellow travelers, and don't lollygag.

17

Baggage Claim

If you have decided not to do battle with the overhead bins, then you will be making your way to baggage claim. But just because you have completed 95 percent of your trip does not mean that you should no longer practice etiquette. The baggage claim area is another concentrated mecca full of anxious fellow travelers. The most common mistake people make is that they all try to congregate, like cattle waiting for the feed pen to open, in the spot where the luggage is discharged onto the carousel. My suggestion is to move farther down the conveyer. This will give you a little more space to maneuver.

If you are meeting someone and you do not need that person's assistance in baggage retrieval, have him or her wait outside the perimeter. This is not a place for extra bodies with nothing to accomplish. Also, I would suggest refraining from using your worthless cell phone. Like other parts of travel, you need to stay focused on the task at hand. Trying to handle the cell phone while grabbing your sixty-pound suitcase will only result in pain and suffering for your fellow travelers.

What invariably happens is the first line of offense will have their knees pressed against the carousel rail, checking every suitcase that looks vaguely familiar. One time, I saw an individual pick up a turquoise cloth suitcase, look at the ID tag, and then place it back on the belt. Next, she picked up a black leather suitcase, checked the ID, and away she went. Either she was drastically color blind, looking to upgrade to a better suitcase, or totally clueless. Most votes came in for the latter.

What's the best method to retrieve your luggage efficiently and courteously? When you spy your suitcase and are not one of the frontline morons, start off with the words "excuse me." This is the polite way to let them know you are reaching in to grab a bag. If you are in the front line and hear these words, kindly move your dumb ass out of the way so this person can keep the procedure moving. Now, when you grab your suitcase and verify it is, in fact, yours, use caution in removing it from the conveyer. Don't knock someone over on his or her butt, shatter his or her kneecap, or set the behemoth down on the person's foot. Keeping your environmental awareness intact, grab your luggage, carefully lift it off the belt, set it on the floor, and then *move out of the way*! This is not the place to repack or

AIRPLANE ETIQUETTE

change outfits. Take your wardrobe and set up camp in a less-crowded area. If you are unable to lift your suitcase because you have packed it full of ball bearings, you need to procure the services of a skycap. Don't expect a fellow passenger to help out.

How about the sign that warns you that the conveyer may start up at any time and to keep children off? Apparently, some people just can't read or don't believe in warnings. During one instance at Los Angeles International, there were three kids playing on the luggage carousel while their parents looked dumbly on. By the way, it was running! And it is not just children who need warning. A well-dressed businessman was flapping on his cell phone with his left leg propped up on the luggage belt. It started up after a warning buzzer and took his foot right out from under him. He did a rather awkward split and then fell down. He managed to catch himself with the hand that was gripping the cell phone. I don't know if it could still receive calls, but the scene was a beautiful bit of ballet.

If your luggage does not appear, maintain your cool. It does happen on occasion. The more you change planes, the better the odds of lost luggage. Most times the luggage comes on an earlier flight, or it will be on the next incoming one. It is rarely lost forever. And nonstop flights are not exempt. I was on a direct flight from Denver to Detroit with a checked bag. It did not come off the baggage belt, but it did arrive on a flight the next day and was promptly delivered to my home fifty miles away. When I inquired as to its journey, a shrug and "these things happen" were all I got.

So the etiquette of travel must continue even after you arrive at your destination. In fact, it is not over yet.

18

Curbside Loading

Hopefully, you have not forgotten the curbside unloading etiquette at the beginning of this book. If you do have short-term memory, please refer back to chapter four. It is also imperative that the people who are picking you up have a clue as to the proper procedures. Curbside loading is just like curbside unloading, just in reverse.

Now you have exited the baggage claim area and are probably scoping out a piece of curb to set up camp. If the stars have all lined up properly, then your ride may be just pulling over at the same time. Since this is rarely the case, let's assume that you will have to wait a brief time. Most airports these days have cell-phone waiting lots where your pickup party can wait for free. You call that person *after* you have your luggage in hand, and he or she drives the short distance to the arrivals.

There is a good chance that between the baggage claim exit doors and the curbside there will be a circus-like atmosphere—anxious dogs released from crates, amped-up smokers trying to get two or three lit, kids running like pent-up hyenas, luggage carts with half of Windsor Castle loaded on them, and, of course, oblivious cell-phone talkers. (They are like cockroaches—they are everywhere!) Carefully scan the curb for available real estate. You may notice that the congestion seems to be a logjam right outside the arriving airline baggage-claim doors. This is because the sheep of the world have no leader. They file outside to the arrival curb like zombies in a B movie. They barely get their selfish asses out of the door before they stop. Meanwhile, the rest of the baggage claimers are being squeezed out to the curb. My suggestion is to check for other exit doors that are less crammed, and use one of them. Then once outside, find a curb area that is less crowded and tell your pickup service the coordinates. Invariably, the rest of the drones will find their soulless way to your waiting area, but at least you will have the curbside advantage.

Now that you have executed your part with etiquette, the real fun begins! Your driver, along with the drivers coming for the wandering wallabies, will soon be approaching, most likely in a state of confusion.

Like curbside unloading, most airports are not designed to handle the glut of aimless automobiles. The simple rule is at least *one* lane must remain open so cars can exit. Seems logical. Not so. Once, I picked someone up at an airport that had four lanes passing through the arrival area. Not one of them was moving. The cause: some butt brain was loading up luggage while parked in the outside lane. And not only was he trying to fit a couple of steamer trunks into a sedan, but everybody got out of the car to hug and kiss the arriving passenger. Meanwhile, the efficiencies of moving traffic through Tampa International were drastically compromised, all because this clueless twit was not practicing etiquette.

So, here is the proper series of events for both the arriving passenger and pickup drivers to make the curbside pickups run smoother. (Not a well-oiled machine—that would be too much to expect.)

The Arriving Passenger

First, find an area that is not as crowded at the curbside Keep an eye out for the pickup car and flag it down when you spot it. Make sure the car has stopped and is in gear (don't laugh), and also check surrounding traffic. One time at O'Hare, an arriving woman was so excited that her boyfriend had finally arrived to pick her up that she dropped her suitcase behind the car trunk and ran to the driver-side door. Well, two things happened next. A car went by her in the adjoining lane and splashed black slush all over her Guccis, and another car slid in behind her boyfriend's and caught her suitcase under the bumper. It was a beautiful series of events! Bottom line: be environmentally aware of the active roadway.

Once the car is securely in place, load your luggage into the appropriate area. If the car has an automatic trunk release, this is a great place to utilize it. If you can load your own luggage and hop into the car without the driver having to get out, you get a gold star for efficiency!

The Pickup Driver

As you arrive into the vortex of arrival traffic, you need to keep an eye out for your pickup, as well as the muttonheads who are jockeying for positions all around you. Luckily, most airport arrival zones are at "creep speed," so reaction time is improved. Once the target has been identified, be as expedient as possible. If your arrival does not need assistance, *stay in the car*! If you can stop, have the arrivals load their luggage and then get in the car—all in under twenty seconds, and then you too will get a gold star for efficiency!

Now that the package has been delivered, you still must maintain some wherewithal to exit the mélange. Those oblivious idiots are still on the premises and will be departing in their usual haphazard way. Only now, they will have the added distractions of hearing all about Aunt Lulu's trip to the Mayo Clinic.

Exit the airport, and find a nice place to stop and have a drink. Then you can hear all about the trip!

19

Conclusion

I HOPE CONGRATULATIONS ARE in order for successfully completing your travels while maintaining *airplane etiquette*. If you did indeed follow the recommendations within this book, then you should be rewarded with a high level of self-respect. If all of your fellow travelers followed the contents of this book, then everyone should have been relaxed and almost euphoric during air travel. The strains of traveling should have been minimal, and you should have enjoyed your trip to some extent. I am not alluding that air travel is like a first-class stateroom on the QEII, but with a little practiced etiquette, it can be more tolerable.

Keep this book handy and refer to it as needed. And by all means, loan it out to someone who is not enlightened. Perhaps some of the guidelines within these pages could even be implemented in other public travel situations, such as the subways, highways, ferry boats, shopping plazas, or almost anywhere that the masses are moving.

We all have had travel horror stories, and they will, no doubt, continue to occur. All of the etiquette in the world can't stop a canceled flight or an unscheduled night in the airport. But when we are moving in the right direction, let's all keep in mind that we are not alone. Make note of your fellow travelers, and hopefully in turn, they will acknowledge your space as well.

Safe and pleasant travels!

Appendix

Airline Clubs

At one point in my travel career, I had access to seven different airline clubs. At the time of this writing, most of those have gone the way of the dodo or have been absorbed through a merger. But the etiquette practices of any airline club will apply to *all* airline clubs. The primary concept to understand is that even though you have paid a membership fee, do not treat the club as your own personal boudoir, or worse, a fraternity party. The same rules of a confined aircraft apply to a clubs environ. You may eat like a sow at home, but here in public, show some restraint. *Clean up after yourself.* I know there are personnel that bus the area, but for God's sake, don't scatter wrappers and crumbs around like a crazed hyena. With cell-phone conversations, talk in low, indoor voices. Most clubs have a designated quiet zone indicating no cell-phone conversations. There will always be the oblivious individual who can't read and calls a long-lost golfing buddy. The best thing to do is politely point out the quiet zone sign. If the violator insists on the conversation, notify club personnel.

Another issue is the art of lounging. If the club is crowded (as most seem to be these days), don't sprawl out and take up valuable chairs for other paying guests.

I have never been a big fan of kids in the club, but if you must expose club members to them, keep them on a short leash, especially around the self-service food areas. I was privy once to a family of five traveling overseas (how they *all* got access is a mystery). Anyway, after they left the club for their flight, it looked like an F5 tornado swept through. The cleaning people needed hazmat suits and a Shop-Vac to clean the debris field. Remember: airplane etiquette extends to airline clubs as well.

Parking Lots

Parking lots, in general, can be intimidating and confusing. Consider the parking lot at your grocery store. Every time you are there, you risk damage to yourself, as well as your car. It all comes down the fundamental understanding of environmental awareness. In a supermarket parking lot, there are cars trying to park, cars backing out of spaces, shopping carts on the loose, and people wandering aimlessly. I recall an incident in a parking lot where a truck with a giant ball hitch attached backed into the side of my car as I was passing behind him. He did not hear my horn, as he was on his cell phone. Hmmmm. Another inept dolt trying to multitask.

So while we were waiting for the police to arrive, a woman across the way gently pushed her cart away from her car, and it picked up momentum and slammed into an unsuspecting Volvo. She did a quick look around and figured no harm, no foul and got in her car and skedaddled. Did I mention that the cart corral was fifteen feet away? There you have a lazy, inconsiderate dumbass. But enough about store parking lots. Just transpose this environment minus the shopping carts to an airport parking garage. Add people running late for flights and the additional multilevels, and you have confusion 101. Much like dropping off or picking up, focus on the task at hand. Turn down the radio, cease conversations, and follow the directional signage (as best that it is). If you are running late, I suggest going to the top floor. You will probably save time, as there are usually more open spaces on the roof. Be a little extra diligent when backing out of a space, as people may be walking behind your car in a state of la-la land. And don't forget where you parked. (I have seen many a returnee on an aimless quest to locate his or her car.)

Shuttles

Most airports have designated areas outside arrival for shuttle pickups. These may include hotel, rental car, between terminals, parking lot, and charters. Taxis may also be bunched in with these. The larger the airport the more congested these areas are likely to be. The best advice is to make sure you are in the correct loading zone. There may be different areas for each type of shuttle (hotel, rental car, etc.). While you are waiting for your particular shuttle, stay clear of other shuttles, so your fellow travelers can board efficiently. The sooner that shuttle leaves, the quicker yours may have an opening for pickup. Now, when it is time to board the shuttle, here is where courtesy kicks in. Allow the passengers who were there *first* to board. Nobody likes a line jumper. If luggage goes in the back, allow the driver to stow it for you. *Do not bring large suitcases on board!* The area inside is for walking, standing, or sitting. Now, some shuttles have luggage storage in the passenger area. In that case, stow your larger suitcases in the designated area, and take a seat. Remember, seats are for butts, not carry-ons. While you are on the short trip to your destination, perhaps you could take a little break from that worthless cell-phone conversation. Like an airplane, shuttles have little personal space. There is a good chance that nobody else on that shuttle will want to hear about your lobotomy. When you do arrive at your destination, I recommend a tip for the driver, especially if he or she helped with your cargo. My basic guideline is a dollar per suitcase, but it is totally discretionary.

Airports

In this section, I want to briefly highlight (and lowlight) some of the top airports within their respective size grouping (large, medium, and small markets). After traveling to or through over 160 domestic airports, I have some firsthand experience as to their attributes and pitfalls. First, I will comment on some of the airports in the large-market category.

Large-Market Airports

Hartsfield-Jackson Atlanta International Airport (ATL): The world's busiest airport in terms of the number of passengers—approximately 250,000 per day. Now, when the "world's busiest airport" is sparking on all cylinders and the weather is cooperating, it is a fine-running machine of movement. However, when there is a weather issue or a capacity problem with air traffic control, the airport gets stuck in the mud. This can have ripple effects across the country on flight departures and arrivals. The eight terminals can also be a daunting stroll from end to end (a little over one mile and one hundred acres). Luckily, there is an interterminal tram.

Chicago O'Hare International Airport (ORD): With approximately 180,000 passengers per day, it is the world's fifth-largest airport in that category. And 82 percent of those passengers are being moved by two hub airlines, American and United. If you happen not to be on either of those two airlines, then O'Hare is a relatively simple airport to navigate. Statistics show that approximately one-sixth of all flight cancellations in the United Sates are at ORD. (The smaller Midway Airport is south of O'Hare.)

Los Angeles International Airport (LAX): Besides the monstrous LAX, there are three other area airports to help with some of the air traffic. But if you are traveling overseas (especially the Pacific Rim), then LAX is the ticket. Its nine terminals handle about 170,000 passengers per day. Changing planes within one terminal is a no-brainer. However, interterminal changes can be a little tenuous. The departures over the Pacific Ocean are viewer friendly.

Dallas/Fort Worth International Airport (DFW): DFW is approximately the same size in area as the island of Manhattan...that puts things into perspective. It has a four-lane highway running through the middle, and even its own zip code. The C-shaped terminals themselves are big enough. If you are unlucky enough to have to change terminals, there is a monorail to move you around. Just pay attention, and leave some time.

Denver International Airport (DEN): DEN is the largest airport in the United States in area, and it hosts the longest public runway. My biggest complaint on DEN is its proximity (or lack thereof) to the city of Denver. When it first opened, there was no such thing as an airport hotel. That situation has greatly improved. The winds coming off the Rockies can make for a roller-coaster landing once in a while.

John F Kennedy International Airport (JFK): This New York airport is the epitome of international exposure. You can pretty much get anywhere in the world without too much difficulty. However, some of the terminals are showing their age.

San Francisco International Airport (SFO): Watch out for morning delays due to fog. If you do get delayed, sour dough bread, *Ghirardelli Chocolate*, and *Anchor Steam* beer can help pass the time.

McCarran International Airport (LAS): If you have a little time to kill, there are plenty of slot machines and video poker in this Las Vegas airport. And speaking of time to kill: plan on having some for the interminable waiting at baggage claim.

Miami International Airport (MIA): Like JFK to Europe or LAX to Asia, MIA is the jumping-off point for the Caribbean and South America. It offers flights heading to islands barely found on a map. It's as close to a Spanish-speaking or Creole-speaking country as you can get without leaving the United States. Both east and west departures/arrivals are scenic, with Biscayne Bay to the east and The Everglades to the west.

Orlando International Airport (MCO): Before the onslaught of Disney and the like, MCO was a hayfield of an airport. However, now it is one of the busiest. Plan on long lines at security and limited overhead bin space (they are usually crammed with stuffed Mickey Mouse toys and such).

Medium-Market Airports

Portland International Airport (PDX): This Oregon airport is all in all an easy airport to navigate. Nice flight approach along the mighty Columbia River. One downside would be that there are no other sizable airports nearby. (Seattle is three hours away, and Eugene is a small-market airport.)

Lambert–St. Louis International Airport (STL): Once the bustling hub of TWA, it is now just a mere reflection of its once-crowded terminals. American Airlines keeps the heart beating by maintaining a minor hub at STL.

Kansas City International Airport (MCI): One of the easiest airports to get from airplane to baggage claim to parking lot with the least amount of steps. It is quite a distance from downtown Kansas City (about twenty miles).

Nashville International Airport (BNA): Keep an eye out for country music stars coming and going.

Cleveland Hopkins International Airport (CLE): A relatively stress-free airport in terms of movement and easy proximity to downtown. There are five alternative airports within one hundred miles of CLE in case you need options.

Memphis International Airport (MEM): It can be a hike from one end to the other. Luckily, there are a few rib-and-beer joints along the way! And at what other airport can you purchase Elvis Presley memorabilia?

Louis Armstrong New Orleans International Airport (MSY): I find the MSY terminals a little dark and crowded...just like Bourbon Street! There are some good eateries tucked in between gates, as well as music.

John Wayne Airport, Orange County (SNA): Keep an eye out for the bronze statue of The Duke in this California airport. A much more manageable airport than LAX

Small-Market Airports

I am going to mention a few *really* small airports. Most of these are only serviced by one, maybe two, commercial airlines. They are extremely easy airports to navigate around.

However, most have limited flights, and a cancellation could mean an extra, unscheduled night.

Muskegon County Airport, Muskegon, Michigan (MKG): Great on-premises restaurant.

Dothan Regional Airport, Dothan, Alabama (DHN): Great for southeastern Alabama and southwestern Georgia travel.

Arcata-Eureka Airport, Humboldt County, California (ACV): Watch out for morning fog delays.

Pocatello Regional Airport, Pocatello, Idaho (PIH): Check out the french fries vending machine.

Northern Maine Regional Airport, Presque Isle, Maine (PQI): It gets dark early in the winter.

Meridian Regional Airport, Meridian, Mississippi (MEI): The nearby military base keeps flights full.

Chippewa Valley Regional Airport, Eau Claire, Wisconsin (EAU): Northwest Wisconsin's airport mecca.

Athens–Ben Epps Airport, Athens, Georgia (AHN): Can get busy during Bulldog football weekends.

Barkley Regional Airport, Paducah, Kentucky (PAH): Servicing the area of the confluence of the Ohio and Mississippi Rivers.

Pitt-Greenville Airport, Greenville, North Carolina (PGV): Gateway to the outer banks.

Delayed/Canceled Flights

The more often you fly the better your chances of experiencing a flight delay or the dreaded flight cancellation.

Delays can occur for a number of reasons. The obvious one is weather. Air traffic control can slow things down due to heavy traffic. Of course, mechanical issues are always a possibility. And my favorite: waiting on the crew.

Cancellations are a little more drastic. Usually, extreme weather or a major mechanical problem will result in a cancellation, especially for smaller airplanes (high winds) and airports (parts may not be readily available). Whatever the reason, true or not, it will do absolutely no good to lose your cool. There is usually one hothead in every situation. I find that after making a complete ass of himself or herself, the passenger gets to his or her destination no quicker than the rest of the inconvenienced travelers. My mother used to say, "You will get further with sugar than with vinegar." So try and be patient and courteous to the gate agents. I can pretty much guarantee the problem is not their fault. They are just the messengers—don't shoot them! Now, I have experienced some gate agents who are just plain pricks. Still try to maintain some decorum, as *your* fate can be in *their* hands. By the way, if the airline offers any type of compensation (and it should), take it. Offers range from food vouchers to hotels to first-class upgrades to full refunds. Air carriers don't have to do much (just get you to your destination in a reasonable time frame), so get what you can. Read the contract of carriage sometime for illumination as to the airlines' responsibilities.

Children on Airplanes

You got to love 'em...but not necessarily on an airplane. I understand the cabin-pressure effect on them, but that usually lasts a brief time. The ones who cause problems are the ones old enough to know better. And actually, it comes down to the parents' lack of discipline. *Kids need to be seated and buckled in.* I don't care how cute you think they are when they are standing on the seat drooling on the passengers behind them (actual experience). Did I mention we were barreling down the runway ready for lift-off? One other comment is that the aisle is *not* a backyard, and the seat in front of the little terror is *not* a kickball!

The airlines need to do a better job of placing families with children or infants in arms. The last thing you want on your Ralph Lauren suit is baby drool from 11A. Perhaps airlines need to consider a no-children section like they used to do with smoking sections.

Elderly and Assisted Fliers

I was taught to always respect my elders, and this holds true when it comes to flying. The airlines, for the most part, have built in ample time to get assisted passengers on board and seated. In fact, on one flight from Detroit to Tampa, I counted sixteen wheelchairs lined up on the Jetway, and we still departed on time. However, one of the inherent problems is with the next batch of fliers (usually first-class or premium passengers). When the airline starts preboarding the passengers needing assistance, the impatient travelers start to horn in on the entryway, much like a Who concert or European soccer game. If they would just back off while the attendants get their jobs done, it would make for a much smoother transition. Now, the airlines are not always righteous when it comes to assisted passengers. On many occasions, I have seen that these fliers have seats way in the back of the plane. It's bad enough that they have to get aboard, let alone walk another three hundred feet to their seat. And one major point regarding elderly/assisted passengers. Upon arrival, there is an announcement to wait in your seats until the rest of the plane has deplaned, when wheelchairs will be available. There is always one elderly or assisted passenger (which usually starts a chain reaction) who insists on getting off with the able-bodied passengers (who may have tight connections). So, Uncle Joe who moves at a snail's pace, do your part, and stay seated!

Flight Attendant Faux Pas

First, don't call them stewardesses (especially the men), and don't *ever, ever* call them waitresses! A gentleman (actually an idiot) called for the "waitress" to bring him another drink. Well, we never saw her again. I was guilty by association on a three-hour flight. The flight attendants' main focus is safety, and, to some extent, to be facilitators. But they are also not without error. I have experienced the following personal faux pas. A flight attendant going into the lavatory and not locking the door...boy, we were both surprised! I have had several

AIRPLANE ETIQUETTE

drinks accidentally dumped in my lap, as well as lunch (luckily, it was a cold plate). A flight attendant left the intercom on while having a personal discussion with another attendant (I didn't know that "that time of the month" was more intense during turbulent weather). On many occasions, the flight attendants, and sometimes the pilot, will tell us we are going to Austin when, in fact, we are going to Charlotte. You can watch the color go out of some people's faces when they hear the wrong destination. Luckily, the crew member is corrected and remakes the correct announcement. One time, the pilot came on the intercom and said, "Thank you for flying Northwest Airlines. It's thirty-two degrees here in Minneapolis, but when we land in Fort Lauderdale, it will be a balmy seventy-eight." That sounded great. However, we were on a Delta flight leaving Milwaukee and heading to Miami. It was a little disconcerting when the pilot made that many errors. He came back on, quickly and smugly, to correct the information (it was right at the time of the Northwest/Delta merger).

Probably the biggest flight attendant faux pas I've witnessed involve the exit-seat row. Flight attendants require a verbal yes that the individual in that seat is willing and able to assist in the event of an evacuation. Once, there was an elderly woman who required a wheelchair. On another occasion there was a large man who I was certain would not fit through the exit door, and then there was the couple from Japan who did not speak English. They all passed the test by muttering yes. Luckily, and as usual, we landed safely without incident.

Printed in Great Britain
by Amazon